SO YOU'RE RETIRING . . .
A GUY'S GUIDE TO BEING AT HOME

So You're Retiring . . .

A Guy's Guide
To Being At Home

William J. Cone

SEABOARD PRESS

AN IMPRINT OF J. A. ROCK & CO., PUBLISHERS

So You're Retiring . . . A Guy's Guide To Being At Home by William J. Cone

SEABOARD PRESS

is an imprint of JAMES A. ROCK & CO., PUBLISHERS

So You're Retiring . . . A Guy's Guide To Being At Home
copyright ©2006 by William J. Cone

Special contents of this edition copyright ©2006
by Seaboard Press

Address comments and inquiries to:
SEABOARD PRESS
9710 Traville Gateway Drive, #305
Rockville, MD 20850

E-mail:
jrock@rockpublishing.com   lrock@rockpublishing.com
Internet URL: www.rockpublishing.com

Paperback ISBN: 1-59663-511-8

Library of Congress Control Number: 2006924287

Printed in the United States of America

First Edition: 2006

For Harriet,
who makes all things
possible and
pleasurable

Contents

Contents

INTRODUCTION

Not everyone wants to, should, or can retire. This guide is for those who do and wish to avoid divorce court. This guide is not for those who have more money than God, a sunny disposition and a wife who adores you no matter what you do.

It is for us middle class dolts, who need a little help navigating the perils of retirement.

You know when you are going to stop. But do you know what you are going to start?

When one retires, working friends and acquaintances are curious as to what it is like. Be careful not to seem too ecstatic with your comments. You may alienate your friends.

HINT: Envy promotes few friendships.

Your spouse's friends will seek her out and ask in a whisper, "How are you doing?" There is fear among some wives of having their husbands "at home". For some, the threat of a husband at home is akin to impending nuclear war. A sense of panic prevails.

Quotes I have heard. "He better not retire. I'm not ready." Or as another friend said, "I married Charlie for better or worse, but not for lunch!"

Your wife has not retired. She is still at home and maybe working outside the home as well. She probably never invaded your workspace. You are now invading hers.

HINT: Tread lightly

When you were working and not around the house, she probably forgave much. She will now expect you to help more. Your help will enable her to "retire" a bit.

An extravagance early in retirement helps to punctuate your release from the work-a-day world. Buy a new car. Take an extended trip. Just be careful that extravagance doesn't become a habit.

If you are a Type A personality or even a Type B, it may take a while for you to realize you don't have to complete each task today. Your desk doesn't have to be clear by five o'clock.

Phone calls don't have to be returned on a schedule, or indeed, at all. "Tomorrow is another day," Scarlet. Kick back and enjoy the slower flow.

When asked by strangers, "What line of work are you in," answer by saying you are unemployed. It starts a more interesting dialogue than by responding that you are retired.

Here's one of the best responses I know from a non-working person when asked what he did for a living.

He said, "Do?"

"Yes, what do you do?"

His response, "Daddy did."

Few of us are that lucky with our parentage.

This guide is just that. It is a way to help you through the maze of problems that can occur in retirement. Humor helps in all situations. Let a smile be your partner as you go forth into the joys of unemployment.

CHAPTER 1

HELP
WITH CHORES

Help her with chores. Are you a help or hindrance? She has her own pace. A friend describes his wife by saying, "She doesn't need a watch, she needs a calendar." Whatever. Just don't try to change her ways.

It's a fine line. Be careful but on her terms. Don't ask her if there is something you can do. Find a project and do it. Perhaps something she has been asking you to do for months. She will like this kind of surprise.

Some Possible Activities

1. Help with the dirty dishes. You wash. She dries or vice-versa. During this time together, it is interesting what you can learn and discuss in this confined space.

In cleaning dirty dishes, technique is important. Your spouse may not agree with an aunt of mine. I used to spend summers with her. She wasn't too fastidious. The first summer, as she was washing and I drying, she said, "Remember the drier gets fifty percent!"

HINT: You can't communicate too much.

---

2 Fill and/or empty the dishwasher. Don't leave dirty dishes on the counter. You can now be one of the kitchen genies that make things disappear. Put things away. Learn where items go. It isn't rocket science.

3. If you are going to help, go all the way. If you are alone at home and fix something to eat, clean up after yourself. One friend's wife calls him slug. He leaves a dirty trail wherever he goes.

4. Clean the tub and shower after you use them. She wants a clean place to bathe and so do you.

5. Make your bed each day. Even learn how to change the sheets. (You may never learn how to remake the bed to her satisfaction, but try.) If you can't, just take a pass and choose another

project. Remember, a favorite quote from W. Somerset Maugham. "Why do American women expect the perfection in their husbands that English women only hope to find in their butlers?"

Even if you are not allowed to make the bed or change the sheets, you can turn down the bed and have the pillows placed for bedtime reading.

**HINT: Thoughtfulness
in any way is appreciated.**

---

6. "Cleanliness may be next to Godliness," and we may "hold certain truths to be self evident," but not necessarily by the recently retired male. Be sure when you use the stove that you clean it. The same goes for keeping the counter tops neat. Wash, dry and put away dishes and pots and pans you use. One couple I know has separate kitchen areas with their own stoves, refrigerators, cabinets and counters. They are only responsible for their own space. The rest of us best toe the line.

**HINT: An ounce of clean
is better than the wife's wrath.**

---

7. Help keep the grocery list. Being home more, you will be raiding the pantry and refrigerator. Be responsible. If you use up an item or if an item is getting low, put it on the list.

8. The night before the trash man comes (or the sanitation engineer, as some like to be called), empty wastebaskets. Tie up papers and magazines. Take it all to the curb.

9. What *are* those white metal things in the basement or utility room? Wherever. Learn that these items are the washer and dryer. The dials look complicated. I still think they are even after using them. But learning new things is supposed to help prevent Alzheimer's. Your wife can teach you. You can learn the correct amount of soap and bleach to use and which settings to dial. Remember, though, if you don't pay attention, you may "suds" the entire area. Learn about separating colors and whites. Don't wash the dog towels with your dishtowels. Don't wash either one with your bath and face towels.

If you have a solar dryer (clothes line to the more prosaic) learn how she likes to pin the clothes. Trust me, she has a system.

It's never too late to change. If you have been putting socks, underwear, etc. in the dirty clothes basket wrong side out, put them in right side out. It will save her time and you too, if you begin to help with laundry. (Not all machines are like the ones we used in college; where they tore the buttons off the shirts and shot them through the socks.) She will love you for it.

HINT: Help more within her perimeters.

If there is a chore you don't like to do, can't do, or the thought of it drives you *crazy*, say so. You are allowed to say no (occasionally). Or, as has been said, "If a job is worth doing, hire someone."

10. Learn to burp the Tupperware. It helps to protect the food. Learn which things go into zip-lock bags and which don't. Learn how to zip-lock them. Some aren't so easy.

11. Don't soak her good cookie sheets. Don't scrub her good pots and pans with an abrasive cleaner or pad.

12. If you are not yet trusted to go grocery shopping, help bring the groceries in from the car. Help to put them away, but not until you learn where and how she likes them arranged.

HINT: You are starting a new job. There is a learning curve.

It takes weeks and sometimes months to establish new routines. Sitting around and just thinking about how to help doesn't work.

HINT: Too much introspection leads to inertia.

---

13. Close windows when it starts to rain. Open them when it stops. God's ventilation system is cheaper than your heat pump. Save the air conditioning for extreme heat.

14. *The Grill*
     A man's place is at the grill. I've never understood the allure. In the first place, it is assumed to be a man's thing to do.

If you like standing around outside in the heat/cold, fighting off bugs/snow flakes, this activity may be your bag. You will have more time to do it now. Scraping and cleaning the thing isn't fun either. There are those who think the fire burns off the last leftover food remnants. I don't think so. If using a grill makes you macho man in your own eyes, go for it. Your wife will love the help. But, please clean the thing when you are finished. Neatness and order are bywords for a happy home.

15. *More About Groceries*

If you do start to help by going grocery shopping remember that this activity is fraught with danger. For at least the first few times go strictly by the list she gives you. No deviation. No smoked oysters. No four-inch filets. You get the picture? You must earn her trust.

Don't be embarrassed to ask a clerk where things are. You can spend hours wandering from aisle to aisle.

16. *Fun at the Checkout Lines*

You will observe that the checkout lanes marked twelve items or fewer are not always the fastest. If you have just run in for some milk and bread, look around. There are grown people who cannot add. Folks in this lane may have forty items or more. Look before you queue up.

Some of these same people never start to look for their credit cards, checks, money or discount cards until all items have been rung up. It's hard to tell who these people will be ahead of time, but with experience a certain prototype will emerge.

Avoid getting behind people with children in tow. Children work as a distraction and add to the time lag. One frustrated mother picked up her pesky little boy and took him to a nearby bench where she sat him down. Hard. He let out a scream. "You busted my balls!" he cried. The area was suddenly quiet. All eyes watched as the little boy stood and removed two smashed ping-pong balls from his back pockets. Episodes are rarely this much fun. But remember, you are unemployed. Be patient. Time is what you have in abundance.

Enjoy observing the human condition. Be glad you are you. However, if you observe some especially irritation characteristics in your fellow man or woman that you occasionally exhibit, it might be time to evaluate your own "human condition."

HINT: Find humor where frustration ruled when you were busy.

---

17. *Lines in General*

Be it the grocery store, banks, going through customs, whatever, I'm convinced there is a gene that allows some people to choose the fast line. I don't have that gene. Hope you do. If not, put your mind in neutral or plan next week's activities. Always have a paperback book in your pocket to read.

CHAPTER 2

WHAT TO DO

1. As you begin your retirement, don't ask your spouse each morning, "What are we going to do today." Your wife is neither your tour director nor your camp counselor. Your happiness in retirement must not depend on her. She has her own schedule, friends and activities. You must develop your programs and routines.

2. Stake out some territory, at home, that is yours alone—den, part of a family room, or maybe a kid's old bedroom. Make it yours. Reach an understanding with your spouse that when you are in this area, your snuggery, as the English call it, you are not to be interrupted. She may have a similar place. Respect

each other's privacy. Marriage is not a fifty-fifty proposition. It is ninety-nine percent with each giving ninety.

3. Consider trips you might like to take with or without your wife.

4. Spend more time with your hobbies. If you don't have any, look around and find some.

5. Think of ways to decrease your taxes. The government wants all of your money. It's up to you to protect what you have.

6. Cut your own grass. You get an exercise bonus. Use a push mower (you save on gas.) Or at least use one with gears to walk behind. Riding mowers are overkill and expensive. They are difficult to store. Unless you mow many acres, you are wasting money. You have time. Cut the grass over several days. What's your hurry? If that type "A" personality is rearing its ugly head, go for the "Best Kept Yard" in the neighborhood award. But only if you want to.

   Do work to keep your yard in great shape. It adds to the "curb appeal." When you get ready to move to a smaller place, your selling price will be enhanced.

7. Everything doesn't have to be done today. You no longer have "in and out" boxes. Let things slide. It feels good, but it does take some getting used to.

8. Have you ever ironed? Don't laugh. Some of us did before we were married. Your wife will love the help. Remember we want to cut down on the laundry cost. Don't pay anyone for work that you can do yourself. The owner of the laundry we use called me several weeks after I retired to ask if he had offended me in some way. I told him no. Why? He said we weren't bringing in as many clothes lately. Yes!! In retirement, you don't need those suits and starched shirts as much. Your lifestyle will change. You can now be Joe Casual. Consider hooking a rug using your ties.

9. Read the paper more thoroughly. Read two papers. Your store of trivia will increase and make you a more interesting person. If your local paper is like mine, you can spend some time correcting the English errors. Send the corrections to the editor. (You might even get a job offer as a proofreader.) I see income potential here.

Don't get in the habit of writing letters to the editor to be published. This activity seems to be addictive and can start hot debates with other readers.

HINT: Retirement is a time for tranquility and peace.

---

10. Learn how to program your VCR and DVR. All the children are usually gone by now. Unless you have grandchildren at home, you need to know how to work this machine.

    Tape old movies or programs that come on past your bedtime (when the rack monster grabs you). This procedure allows you to view these programs during the day. Most commercial daytime T.V. is inane and not for the retiree. It's for the brain dead.

    Tape programs you like and she doesn't. Tape when two programs you like are on at the same time. Watch these programs at your leisure. You have plenty of it now. By recording programs, you can fast forward through the commercials and those three-hour movies only take about two hours.

11. Learn to vacuum and dust. You might like the order it brings to your home. She will be astonished and happier.

12. Go to the post office to mail packages and to get stamps. Run errands. Put gas in the cars. Have the oil and tires checked. Few women like to pump gas.

13. Take courses. Develop new horizons. One friend took up painting and this hobby *required* that he take classes in Mexico (whatever works!). Remember those classes you wanted to take in school, but couldn't for various reasons? Now is the time to take them, be it art, history, photography or woodworking. Your local colleges and technical school will allow you to audit courses and very often, after the age of sixty or sixty-five, there is no fee. There is also no report card, no pass/fail. There is also the potential benefit of meeting new and interesting people.

14. Clean out the shed, attic, basement, storage areas, etc. You may find trea- sures—your old catcher's mitt. You will certainly find spider webs and creeping things. If you haven't used something in

over five years, you probably won't.
Throw it out or give it away. If you have
many such possessions, consider a
garage sale. Money made from junk is
especially welcome.

15. Organize your dresser drawers and
closets. Begin to weed out what you
don't need or want. Do you really need
those four dozen T-shirts with tennis,
golf or marathon logos?

16. How about those pants with a size 30
waist, now that you are a size forty?
Unless you develop (God forbid) a lin-
gering debilitating illness, you will
never be a size 30 again! These items
can help cloth someone less fortunate
and perhaps earn you a tax credit.

17. If you have collected books and magazines through the years or have a large
CD or record collection then evaluate
them. Save what is worthwhile and put
these things in order. If your mother
didn't throw away all of your comic
books, you might find a treasure. The
same goes for that old Lionel train
boxed in the basement.

18. Start or join a club. One senior tennis
team I know about is called the Meta
Mucils. A good self-image is required for

membership. There is fishing, hunting, golf, gardening, and an inexhaustible number of things to do. Get started!

Bet many of you have an old coin, baseball card, or stamp collection you started years ago. Check it out. You may find some value, or best of all, you might ignite a spark of interest to start collecting again.

If you live near a body of water, consider getting a boat. But, remember this sage advice: "The two happiest days of a boat owners life is the day he buys it and the day he sells it."

19. *Home Maintenance*

Paint and mend fences. Seal decks and walkways. If you are not handy with such projects, do some research and find the best deals from the best people. It takes time, but you are the Master of Your Time. Beware of recommendations that state, "He's very expensive, but he's worth it." Yeah, right! How about, "He's very good and reasonable." Check out work he has done. You have time. Talk with previous customers.

20. Be civil to your spouse. Carping old people aren't pleasant to be around.

Don't forget to say "please" and "thank you." Hold her chair at the table (even at home). When you leave or enter a room, give her a pat or hug.

HINT: Even small good deeds and courtesies help to negate big blunders that can occur in retirement.

---

21. *Cull, Cull, Cull*

We are not immortal, despite what my mother use to think when she would say, "If I die ..." Believe me folks. It's gonna happen. If you have ever had to empty a house or apartment after a family death, you know how difficult and frustrating it can be. What do we keep? What should go to the dump? What goes to Goodwill? Worn-out under-wear is no problem, but what about that bowl? Is it a dime store copy or an eigh-teen-century original?

Money and jewelry have been found in the toes of shoes. Stock certificates and uncashed dividend checks lie in wait among old newspapers and magazines. Clean and put order to your own house. Don't put your loved ones through this ordeal.

22. Prepare a list of the important people and places in your life. Who is your lawyer, accountant, broker, executor of your will, insurance agent, banker? What are their addresses and phone numbers? What credit cards do you have? Where are your insurance policies? Do you have safety deposit boxes? Where are the keys? Which bank are they in? Where are your checking and savings accounts? Who has the mortgage on your home? Where is the title if you own it? The same goes for your cars. To compile this list isn't difficult. It must be done! Now!! Tomorrow may not be "another day" for you. Keep a copy at home. Let your family know where it is. Have a copy in your safety deposit box and your lawyer should have a copy. Hop to it.

23. On a gentler note, why not start or join a lunch club with retired friends? The best name for such a group that I have heard is "The Romeos"... retired old men eating out. Bet you can come up with an equally good acronym.

   Such a meeting of unemployed folks gives one an opportunity to exchange ideas and offers a time to ventilate frustrations. Your friends may have already solved the problems you are having. Consider taking an "about to be" retired friend to lunch. You can help to educate him about some of the perils and joys.

24. Go to movies in the afternoon. It's cheaper, less congested and don't forget your senior citizen discount. (In England they call us OAPs...old age pensioners. Has a better ring, doesn't it?)

25. Dig out all of those old photographs and label them. Bet even now you can't name all the people in them.

26. Clean out your wallet at least yearly. It reduces the bulge in your pocket and you are better able to find items when you need them.

CHAPTER 3

THINGS
TO AVOID

It's good for you to organize your sports equipment and help with the shopping. Just don't try to organize your wife's possessions or activities. It probably can't be done and divorces are expensive.

Don't interfere with her household routines. Learn what they are and find ways to help.

There are areas where she will be very territorial. It is her home ground. Learn what is verboten and what isn't. Remember, she didn't tell you what to do at work.

Discuss and avoid the "He's going hunting so I get a new freezer syndrome." If such a pattern already exists, try to modify it. You may be doing lots of "away from home activities" in retirement. (Just don't try taking female company with you.) As your wife thinks about it, your absence may be just the break she needs. Sometimes a little less togetherness isn't a bad thing. One spouse I know loves these opportunities to "veg out," eat tuna fish sandwiches, and watch videos.

In retirement, you and your wife must become a team, not competitors. A new relationship must be forged. Two of you are at home now. Expectations and realities must be confronted and blended.

She may want you to start doing some things she doesn't like to do. Her "to do" (honey do) list can be irritating. Talk about it, but remember, you have the time. Don't say no just to mark your territory. Lighten her load and lift her spirits. You will both profit. You want peace and happy times in retirement. She does too. Work it out.

HINT: Never go to bed
mad at each other.

If you choose to do nothing more than sit and stare at the walls, do it away from her sight. Idle men in view of working women can cause them to become overwrought.

HINT: "When mama ain't happy,
ain't nobody happy."

You may have been used to giving orders at work. Don't try it at home. My wife once told me, "You would be very good with servants. It's a shame you don't have any." Be alert for other subtle hints. I once forgot an outing my wife and I had planned. There were no recriminations. Just a colorful card in the mail of beautiful birds on the cover saying, "The birds are for you" and on the inside, "and vice versa." I never forgot again.

HINT: Even old dogs can be taught.

The question of yard work may come up. If you don't know a pansy from a maple tree, you might want to take a pass on this opportunity. If you think you may have found a new activity then attend classes offered (for free) at most garden centers. There is satisfaction in digging in the dirt and growing things. Try it. You might like it.

There are unspoken rules. She knows these rules. You do not. She has a place for everything. You can upset her by not adhering to the unknown rules. Ask and learn. If she leaves drawers and doors open and it bothers you, don't make an issue. Close them. Live and let live.

If she says, "You're being too helpful" then back off. What she really means is that you have overstepped into her territory. Don't get mad.

Take the dog for a walk.

Listen and learn. These are your platinum years (if you still have hair). Find out what threatens her role. We all tend to be protective of our turf. Do you want her straightening up your tools?

After your bride has finished talking on the phone, don't ask to whom she was speaking. If she wants you to know, she will tell you. (*Exercise caution here.* It may also irritate her that you aren't interested enough to ask.) The same rules apply to your phone conversations. Volunteer the information if you wish, but you need to respect each other's privacy.

However, if you answer the phone during the day and a man's voice asks, "Is the coast clear?" you might want to determine whether your phone number is similar to that of the weather bureau.

The commodity you have in abundance now is free time. *Beware.* Lots of people want to spend it for you:

"You're not working? Great! You are perfect for this project." (Translation — "We haven't found anyone to take it yet.")

"Oh, come on. Don't be a leech on the community. Get *involved.*"

"Just agree to be on our board. It only meets once a month." Naturally, they forget to tell you about the two or three required committees you must also join — that meet weekly. Then there are the fundraisers and special events to promote the organization.

If you are a type "A" or "AA" personality then this kind of activity may be your cup of tea. Go for it. Other groups will notice and you will be in great demand. You may even receive the Volunteer of the Year Award.

However, if you don't need to be wanted and used, run for your life and your free time.

The haggling that can occur among board members, often over the most trivial things, may not be conducive to a healthy stomach lining or your mental health. When you were working "you have been there and done that" with these situations. Do you really want to travel this road again? At this juncture, you're not even being paid for it. Forget it! Spend more time in your hammock.

Just thank these good folks kindly and say for your first year or so of retirement, you just want to evaluate your options. If they begin to push you about their project, just say, "I'm all right, Jack."

It has been said that "Life begins when the children leave home and the dog dies." If you don't have an animal at retirement time, DON'T GET ONE! One of the big joys of the unemployed is the ability to just pick up and go. Making arrangements for your animal is rarely easy, often costly, and just one more problem to avoid.

Consider a "time share dog" or cat. Talk with friends who have pets you like and offer to care for them when your friends leave town. You will be doing a great service and derive pleasure at the same time. Think of it as your warm and fuzzy interlude.

HINT: Uncomplicate your life.

CHAPTER 4

WAYS TO SAVE MONEY

Clean out the basement and attic. Don't rent storage lockers. Throw away things no one wants or needs but remember your trash may be someone else's treasure. Consider having a garage sale. However, your collection of paper bags and "bits of string too small to use" must go.

Offer items to your children. If they are just setting up housekeeping, they may want some things they have rejected before. If they don't want them then don't get mad. Get rid of them. (The items, not the children.) If you empty a commercial storage locker and sell the contents, you have made money twice. No more rent to pay and money in your pocket. Do it!

For entertainment, attend free lectures. You might even learn something! Every town usually has some kind of lecture series. They may even want you to speak if you have an area of interest that fits their format.

Computers are a problem. I might even say they are an addiction for some. If you have a computer and love it, it can certainly fill your free time. On the other hand, if you don't know a thing about computers then think twice before buying one. It's a bit of a money pit. Something new is always needed to upgrade it. It isn't fast enough. How fast do you need? You're not going anywhere. You're retired!

These same thoughts apply to Palm Pilots. The point of retirement is that you DON'T NEED TO BE ORGANIZED! How busy can your schedule be? If you really need a Palm Pilot or some such gadget, someone or many someones are using YOUR free time. Check it out.

Cell phones can be useful when you are traveling and need road help. They are handy for moving about in the house and yard. Spend some time investigating and comparing the cost and service between the cordless landline and cellular phone. Jumping up to answer a "fixed" landline phone may be a form of aerobic exercise but at retirement our "jumper" doesn't always work well. Broken bones are expensive. You know never to use one while driving. Keep both hands on the wheel. Distractions can kill. I saw the ultimate stupid not long ago. A man was reading a book propped on the steering wheel while he proceeded down the freeway at sixty-five miles per hour! "Hell ain't half full yet." Or, as a favorite billboard of years past stated, "Are you on the road to kingdom come?" Don't shorten your leisure years.

About Phones

Caller ID can be useful if you are discriminating as to whom you wish to speak and when. Call waiting is another matter. If someone really wants to talk with you or has something important to say, they will phone back later. It is plain rude to stop talking with one person when another person calls. Especially if you think the second call is more worthy. The first caller is often miffed and rightly so. Both systems increase your phone bill.

About Computers and Technology

Why must every new technology, like the computer, develop its own language? Some of it is downright silly. Why say "log on" instead of "turn on"? And what on earth is a "giga" and why does it bite? Words like hard drive, soft drive and floppy (at our age, we don't like this last term) require deciphering. If I want to learn a new language, I shall, at least, choose one that helps me to find a bathroom while traveling in Europe.

Find out the cost of these things, including all the bells and whistles the salespeople say you need. (How many ram...are we talking sheep here? Are we going to have to go to shepherd school?) Think about other uses for your money...more wine, more trips. Is a computer really worth it?

Let us not even consider cybersex. But it does have one distinct advantage over the "old fashioned kind." You're not likely to get any sexually transmitted diseases.

I haven't figured out yet why you need a Christmas card list on a computer since you already have this information in your address book. The same goes for transferring recipes. "But it opens up the whole wide world of cyberspace." I take in more information than I can process now.

If you have a computer and love it or just must have one, it is, of course, your choice. Use it to search for the best deals on airline tickets, hotel rates, car prices, etc. Don't buy one for these reasons. Have a friend search for you. Folks love showing how good they are in cyberspace. Send them a postcard from your travels.

Many companies assume everyone has a

computer and only give their dot com or org address in ads. Silly companies. They are missing the forty to fifty percent of us who use the telephone. How hard is it to print a phone number as well?

Perhaps their point is that there is no one to answer a phone. Pity! If there is a phone, please, Lord, don't let it be one of the unending voices that want you to punch one through infinity for what service you want. In this circumstance, what you really want to punch is the idiot who bought this program.

Fax machines and shredders are also superfluous. Use a friend's fax on those rare occasions you need one. Take him a bottle of wine for his trouble if you are becoming a nuisance.

The post office still does a fairly good job of getting information from point A to point B. For the money saved, you can forget instant gratification.

Matches are cheaper than shredders and will destroy your credit card numbers and old bank statements. You really don't have nuclear secrets to protect.

Unless health problems dictate the need for an organized regimen of exercise, forget the gym. You can get enough exercise working around the house and yard. Walking in your neighborhood helps to reduce stress and has been found to relieve depression. You have the added advantage of seeing what your neighbors are doing.

We are old. Retirement age is often fifty to sixty-five. This time frame is *not* middle age. How many one-hundred to one-hundred-and-thirty-year olds do you know? Work out to develop a six-pack of abs at this age? You've got to be kidding. You have seen the ads of these people. Old men with muscles are grotesque. A good self-image is one thing. Self-delusion is quite another.

If a new car is to be a retirement treat, consider one that gets good mileage and has a large trunk. You will be taking trips. Save that gas money. Let's face it, just about all cars look alike. Original styles and distinctive brands went out the door in the fifties. Forget the prestigious name brands. You have retired. You have made it. Let the wannabes keep up with the Jones'. They are still working.

HINT: A gallon saved is more food and drink for you.

If there are two of you, you don't need three or more cars, trucks, RV's, etc. Consolidate. Two are enough, or perhaps even one. If you occasionally need another type of vehicle, borrow or rent it.

Do not, under any circumstances, have a motorcycle. (Murdercycles, as friends have called them.) If you have lots of life insurance and a superb health care policy to cover a vegetative or paralytic state and you already have a motorcycle, then carry on. But why try to shorten your last number of earthly years?

How about your house. Is it big? Is it too big now that the children are gone? Think about the taxes and upkeep. Even if you don't have a mortgage, think smaller house, smaller yard. "But the kids need a bedroom when they come home." Phooey! Have one spare bedroom, if you must, for friends and relatives. If you need more space, on occasion, you can put these folks up at a motel or Bed and Breakfast. (Then you don't have to get up early to feed them.) This solution is much cheaper than keeping a lot of empty bedrooms most of the time. (I suppose you could take in boarders.)

The money tied up in your house can be invested and used to put a golden ring around your platinum years. Currently, there is a tax advantage to selling a home if you have lived in it two years or more. In gearing down, it also allows you to reduce your possessions so that chore doesn't fall to your heirs.

How about that second or third house or condo you might have? These extra homes can certainly use up some of your time, but often in ways you don't appreciate. They receive wind and rain damage. They need new paint and per-

haps a new roof. The plumbing leaks. If you rent
or lease these places when you aren't using
them, you have another headache with upkeep.

An exception to not owning a second home is
when you buy a small place for your retirement
while you are still working. You can rent this
property, make tax deductible improvements
and have it paid off when you move in after you
receive your gold watch.

HINT: Plan, Plan, Plan.

Rethink season tickets to anything. If you
really attend all of the events and love them,
keep buying. But, if on evaluation, you realize
you don't go enough to justify the cost, stop the
subscription. Just because you have bought
them for twenty years while you were working,
is no reason to continue. Buy only as needed.

HINT: Reevaluate, Rethink.

**Cut Out Unnecessary and
Unwanted Money-Draining Activities**

1. There is no reason to continue to pay
   yearly dues for professional member-
   ships. Your profession now is to relax
   and save money.

2. Do you really read and enjoy all the magazines and newspapers that come to your home? CULL!! Read them at your local library.

3. Being at the library also serves the purpose of getting you out of the house and out from under the feet of your significant other.

4. For heaven's sake, don't waste money buying clothes with some company's logo. If you are paid to advertise their product, fine, but don't pay extra for the privilege.

5. Don't buy books. Your library is filled with them and generally gets all the current best sellers. Even when you return them overdue, we oldsters often have the charge waived.

6. Compare the cost and function of cable T.V. to satellite.

7. If you still belong to clubs that have a lunch or dinner meeting, consider how many of these you actually attend. If you are charged, regardless of attendance, then these clubs may be more habit than an enjoyment.

8. Don't just belong to things in order to "fluff up" your obituary. These organizations can still be listed as "past member of." Are you really going to care in the hereafter? Save the money for fun while you are "here and now."

9. Barter. If you do carpentry and a friend knows plumbing, help each other out. Start a project together.

10. Don't go to movies often. If the film is any good, or popular, it will be on video soon. It is much cheaper to view at home (with as many people as you want) and so is the obligatory popcorn and Cokes. If your eyesight is so bad you think you need the big theatre screen, just move closer to your television set.

To sum it up, a wise friend once put it succinctly. "We practice everyday thrift so that we can enjoy the occasional extravagance.

HINT: Viva La Thrift!

CHAPTER 5

TRAVEL

Taking a trip is often at the top of the list of things to do in retirement. It is especially appealing if you haven't had time to do much before.

The planning is almost as much fun as the trip, but tread carefully. Your idea of a great trip may be Dante's third level of hell to your spouse. Talk. Listen. Work it out. Don't be like the song Professor Higgins sings in "My Fair Lady" where he and she want different things and compromise by doing something that neither likes.

Check for the best rate. You are now flexible with your time. At hotels, which part of the week is cheaper? Are there midweek or weekend specials? Is breakfast included? Is there a refrigerator and/or a microwave in the room?

When making hotel/motel reservations, companies want to give you a confirmation number. Beware. A confirmation number is just that, a number. What they put into their computer under that number may not be what you want. Mistakes can happen. If you don't have a letter from them stating what kind of accommodations and the dates you want them, you have no proof of the reservation you desire. Been there. Been had. Get the details in writing.

A number is a number is a number only!

Your library may have CDs and tapes to check out. Utilize this under-used resource. Books on tape are great for those trips you will be taking. The library CDs work well in your car and offer different music from what you have at home...at no cost.

If you want to spend some time in a favorite city, consider renting an apartment or condo for several weeks or months. It is much cheaper than hotels and allows you many options. The main problem with the renting idea is finding a source for this information in your desired city. Perseverance will pay off.

A word about eating out on these trips. Great restaurants are just as great at lunch. Chefs may change from lunch to supper, as Anthony Bourdain points out in *Kitchen Confidential,* but generally not. The cost is anywhere from one-third to one-half less at lunch. Your stomach will enjoy a great meal whenever you have it. Wine with lunch may make you sleepy. Good. Go back to the apartment and take a nap. Naps are wonderful.

Grocery shop and cook an easy meal for supper. Soup and a sandwich on a great local bread are ideal. Make some guacamole. Vary your culinary experience. Breakfast is always easy. It can be very simple, especially if you have lunch out.

If you fly to your destination, don't feel you must rent a car; always an expensive proposition. You won't use it as much as you think. Reserve renting a car for those out-of-the-area excursions. Public transportation is cheap. You see more while riding on a bus or streetcar. In some places, you can buy a weekly or monthly transit pass and save even more money.

Wander around your city and discover out-of-the-way places and fun areas in which to walk. Check the local newspaper for current happenings. We discovered, in one city, that the admission to museums is free on the first Monday and Tuesday of each month. With the money saved you can get a super lunch at the museum café. Really, the food in museums is imaginative, delicious and quite reasonable. Then you don't have to cook much for the evening meal. At a museum lunch, you can feed your face and your soul at the same time.

Visiting relatives or attending family reunions can cause concern and conflict. If you enjoy this type of activity, no problem. If one of you doesn't like to do it, the issue should not be forced. One or the other of you may want to see the relatives every five or ten years, but yearly or more frequently certainly isn't necessary. Be flexible and don't pout about it. If you want to go, go alone. Don't let it be a source of conflict.

The same goes for class reunions. Unless your spouse attended the same school as you did, she probably has absolutely nothing in common with these people. At this point in time, you may not either.

The people who have the most fun at these things were the head cheerleader and the star quarterback. Even in their wrinkled and overweight condition, they, no doubt, have better memories of the years past than you do. (No Virginia, life isn't fair.)

If you have a trophy wife, number two, three, or four, it may well be part of your program that she accompany you. After all, it is part of the reason you married her. Show her off. She will like the attention. In this situation, if you don't already have a fire engine red sports car convertible, rent one! Go all the way, but please DON'T have your ear pierced.

At one "thirty something" reunion, when each person was asked to stand and give a brief synopsis of his life and family, one fellow said he had a thirty-two-year-old daughter. The emcee asked if anyone had a child older than thirty-two? In the ensuing silence, a wag in the back asked, "Does anyone have a wife older than thirty-two?" Not everyone laughed.

CHAPTER 6

TAXES, FINANCES (SINS OF OMISSION)

Time to tackle these sins of omission. The excuse you have used about not having enough time to do these things no longer applies. Get off the dime and get started.

You are not immortal. Get with the program. Make some hard decisions. Who gets what? Clean up your financial house. Doing so makes it easier on you. Planning can give you and your heirs more money than you thought you had.

Taxes

In retirement, despite what you may have been told, taxes may take more of your money than anticipated, especially if your state suddenly imposes an income tax.

Are you paying too much tax? Of course you are. The government (local, state and federal) thinks it knows better how to spend your money than you do. Spend more time with an accountant to see if you can reduce your tax bite. Find out from which accounts (savings, IRAs, CDs) you should be taking money to live and play on.

These thoughts bring to mind the concept of an Estate Planner. There are more Estate Planners than Carter has pills...some good, some bad, some indifferent. Which one to choose? God only knows. Search. Ask your friends to recommend. Has he made any money for them? Interview some. Compare cost.

Decide what your goals are. Do you love the government so much that you want it to get most of your money when you die? If so, you don't need to do anything. If not, work to reduce estate taxes to as close to zero as possible. There are many charities that are better run to distribute your money than Uncle Sam. Put your insurance policies in a trust. Set up trusts for your children, grandchildren, or a home for pregnant cats. You don't have to be a millionaire to protect your assets.

Evaluate your IRAs in reference to their tax implications. Should they be changed to a different kind? Should you continue to fund them? Ask questions.

Make sure your spouse will have money to

use as soon as you die. (She should do likewise.) Probate can take a long time. Check out your joint accounts and joint stock holdings. Look into a mechanism called "transfer on death" for stocks. You will never learn all the ins and outs of saving and protecting your money, but unless you try, you will certainly be losing some money you shouldn't.

Get your real-estate ownership in the appropriate names and/or trusts for minimal estate taxes. Take advantage of any and all loopholes. Knowledge is power.

Evaluate your insurance policies. Do you have any? Do you have enough? Do you have too many? Are they vulnerable for estate taxes? Let us make the effect of our death on our survivors as inexpensive as possible. Save that money for more whiskey at the wake!

As you retire, if you are under age sixty-five, try to stay on your company's health plan. Individual policies are outrageous and will about suck your wallet dry. To not have health insurance coverage may be a money saver, but it is a sleep loser. In the long haul, it is the rare person who doesn't get sick or have an accident. The act of just living past sixty causes our bones to crumble, if we don't take certain measures.

If you have a personal articles floater with your insurance policy, reevaluate it. Are you paying to protect items that spend ninety percent of the time in a safety deposit box? Think about it. Will your bank waive the yearly fee on your safety deposit box if you are a good customer? Ask them.

Consider long-term care insurance. Unless you have *lots* of money, an extended debilitating illness will break the bank. Search for the best deals. Make sure the policy includes home *and* nursing home care.

Medicare

It's certainly not the complete answer to your prayers but it is cheaper than an individual policy. Hooray for being sixty-five. You will still need to consider supplemental insurance to go with Medicare. Prices can vary, as can benefits. Get the most for less.

The best old age "bene" is Social Security. It's really wonderful to, at long last, begin to get some of "your money" back. Had you been allowed to invest all the money taken from you, you would have a lot more in your golden years. On the other hand, you might be a poor investor and have ended up with little or nothing.

There is nothing wrong in starting to collect Social Security at age sixty-two, when possible. It takes twelve years to make up the difference in benefits if you have waited until age sixty-five to collect it. Are we going to be around at age seventy-seven? Possibly not and you would have missed this income supplement for three years. Learn as much as possible about how to manage your assets.

HINT: No one is as interested in your money as you are.

Question and ride herd on your money. If one strategy isn't working, try another. Cover bases for up and down markets. Don't get carried away and spend more than usual in the fat years. There are always lean years to follow. At this stage of your life, you don't have ten to twenty years for a losing plan to "turn around." Always look for hidden cost, time restrictions and penalties for withdrawing your money when you invest in CDs, annuities, etc.

In retirement, money makes the difference between a fun time or a time to panic. Some folks enjoy being a greeter at Wal-Mart. You might be one of them. But don't permit yourself to be put in a "have to" position.

HINT: PLAN, PLAN, PLAN.

Someone asked me how long I had been planning to retire. My answer, "Since I started work." You can't start too early.

CHAPTER 7

PERSONALITY AND BODY ADJUSTMENT

A friend's mother once said, "As we grow older, we become more like ourselves." A condensation of our good and bad traits. God help us! That's a scary thought.

Unless you have been nominated for sainthood (and who wants to live with one of those), consider past behavior and attitudes. See if increased civility will help to create a more pleasant home atmosphere. Work on your personality and body with the same vigor you work on your finances.

Drink more water. Old and young tend to be dilatory in this department. More water helps to create better skin, helps to curb our appetite, acts as a diuretic, prevents urine infections and aids the digestive process. It's cheap. Get with the program. Feel better and live longer.

With time, our hearing diminishes. Conversations can be missed or misconstrued. Don't talk to each other from different parts of the house. Talk while in the same room. It's fussy. It's frustrating, but it works for better communications.

It's not just our countenance that changes with time. Our internal parts decide to change as well. It's not uncommon to become sensitive to such things as nutrasweet, monosodium and lactose. You may think that you have an iron belly, but with time all things change. Our immune system can alter. An aunt of mine, became sensitive to scotch in her golden years. She didn't join AA, she quickly switched to bourbon.

HINT: Where there is a will, there is a way.

Rarely do any of our senses become more acute with age. Make sure you and your spouse tell each other about stains and spots on clothes. You don't have to be homeless to look like a street person. Be vigilant. Be a "helpful observer."

At our age, going up and down stairs can be a challenge in itself. Please hold onto the banister. Our feet lose their memory sometimes and we tend to misstep.

HINT: Protect those bones.

If we are honest with ourselves, we know that when we are sick we are always sicker than our wives. It's a guy thing. With no work schedule to keep this "poor me situation" in check, we must try to get better sooner and to whine less. After knee surgery, my bride gave me a bell to ring if I needed her. She also gave me a hard stare and said, "Don't abuse the privilege."

HINT: Lines of behavior can be drawn.

Other Self-Improvement Projects

Look around. A good retirement project is to lose weight. Have you ever seen so many fat people? Are you part of this group? We like to rationalize our weight and eating habits. "I eat like a bird." (Yeah, two and half times my weight each day.) "It's glands." "My father's family is all fat." "It's heredity." No, it's mostly baloney. The kind you eat. Take charge of your diet. Spend more time learning about good nutrition. You probably won't have a twenty-eight inch waist again, but you also don't have to put three hundred pounds on your five foot eight inch frame.

HINT: He, who lives by the calorie, dies by the calorie.

Shape up. You will live longer and feel better. Medicine you don't have to buy leaves money in your bank account. I have always wondered how many overweight people on cholesterol, diabetes, and blood pressure medicine would need these medicines if they lost weight and got in shape. How many orthopedic problems and painful joints might be better if they didn't have to carry so much weight?

Situations that have caused you stress during your working years no longer need to be a problem. For instance: Waiting for the bank teller at the drive-through window. Observe those in front of you. It is similar to the folks in the grocery store line. (In fact, it's probably the same people.) They don't begin reaching for their wallets, making out their deposit slips and fumbling for their savings pass books until they reach the teller. Enjoy and laugh. You have time now. There are no deadlines unless that nasty type A personality has reared its ugly head. Laughter is good for your soul and your good physical and mental health.

If you are the compulsive type, you might be spending more of your time straightening pictures, rugs and your towels. Chill out! You can't be that bored, or it might be time to visit your friendly physician and talk about Prosaic or Zoloft.

Say yes to drugs, when they can brighten your emotional load. Your friends will be happier to have you around. You will be happier in your own skin. Your mind, body and finances all need to be fine-tuned so that you can enjoy the leisure for which you have worked so hard.

CHAPTER 8

MORE WAYS
TO SPEND TIME

Naps are good and come in several sizes. There is the quick after lunch nap. You may have even enjoyed this type while working; providing you are one of those people who can be refreshed and not feel drugged after a fifteen- or twenty-minute respite. Now that you are unemployed, you can nap for one to two hours after lunch. Just don't let it run over into cocktail time!

There is the nap before going out in the evening. This nap is best taken in the late afternoon. It may last an hour or more. When you awake, it will be time to bath, shave and dress. These activities will help to wake you up. This nap will prevent you from falling asleep at someone's dinner table. I do "get too hungry (and sleepy) for dinner at eight." A "toes up," as the English say, helps to alleviate this problem.

Nap when it is raining. The sound of rain on the roof, the wind through your room lets you hunker down and enjoy the good life.

Nap in a hammock. Have a table alongside to hold a book, beverage and radio. To quote an old ad, "It doesn't get better than this."

A corollary to taking naps is the sleeping late theme. You don't have to be anywhere at seven, eight or nine. Log some rack time. This activity may be difficult to clear with the distaff part of your home, but can still be fun on occasion. Having breakfast in your pajamas and robe is another way to punctuate your newly acquired freedom. If you sleep in the "all together," wear a robe to the table. Your wrinkles may spoil her appetite.

Read more of the newspaper. Check out the personals and advertisements. Who knows what you might find.

Enjoy being at home when the mail comes. Write more letters to your children, friends and relatives. You will receive more mail. You can read a letter anywhere. E-mail ties you to your computer. Is that computer chair really as comfortable as other furniture in your home?

Be careful what you write to children in college. We discovered years later that our children posted our letters on their dorm doors for the amusement of their friends. They started a trend at two schools. A friend told me she knew she was "becoming her mother" when she caught herself writing to her children about: (1) What was growing in the yard; (2) Whom she had seen at the grocery store; and, (3) What the weather had been.

Let's face it. Few of us are candidates for a Pulitzer Prize, but it is fun to receive mail no matter how prosaic. Your friends and family will know you care.

Start a compost bin. You will be recycling plant and fruit products that will help to make your garden and flowers grow.

If you like to eat (and who doesn't) take some cooking classes or utilize your library again and check out cookbooks. Try new recipes. If you clean up your dishes, your wife probably won't mind your invasion of her kitchen, especially, if she doesn't have to cook dinner.

Start a dinner club with friends. Or, just call friends and say you have a main course, if they have a salad and/or dessert. "Bring it over and let's eat!"

HINT: Spending more time with friends is a bonus of retirement.

Enjoy knowing that you rarely have to wear a tie. That top shirt button is no longer needed. There are many kinds of freedom.

Remember, you are not working. You have no deadlines. Don't create any for yourself or allow others to do so. Smile baby. You have made it!

CHAPTER 9

TIGHTEN FINANCES

Never, ever, allow yourself to pay interest on a credit card. You need all the money you have saved through the years. If you can't afford to pay off the items you buy each month, do without them. There are millions of people throughout the world who are "doing without." You can, too. Let the credit card companies make their money from someone else.

In fact, try and get a "no fee" credit card. Also get one that allows you to accumulate frequent flier miles. Travel and the time to do it are two of the great joys of retirement.

Use discount cards at the grocery, pharmacy, anywhere you can. Then charge the cost on your frequent flier no fee card.

Charge everything possible on your travel card: groceries, gas, clothes, restaurant bills, lawn mowers and everything you buy. If you can buy a car for cash, try putting it on your card for the miles. It has been known to work, or, at least, part of the price. Your car cost may give you wings.

Use plain vanilla checks. You really don't need "deluxe checks" with a picture of your dog or a seacoast scene. Plain is cheaper and works just fine. You will have the need for fewer checks by using your no fee credit card. But

PAY IT OFF EACH MONTH!

Consider having certain bills e.g. electric, water, gas, insurance premiums paid directly from your bank. Sometimes these can also be charged to your credit card. (Can't you just feel yourself getting closer to that trip to Europe or the Orient?)

It scares me, a bit, that others have access to my bank and credit card numbers, but that is the choice we must make. Another way to look at it is, that as we become "more mature," we become more forgetful. The automatic payment of these bills will prevent late charges. It is also a good system if you are out of town for long periods of time.

Your laundry and dry cleaning bills will generally be lower when work stops. You have fewer reasons to dress up. Now, don't get odoriferous. Just do more washing at home.

Do you have a second or third home or investment property? Do you really need or want them? Are they cost effective? Were they just for a tax write-off while you were working? Put the pencil to the paper. What is your death tax liability with these properties; especially, if they are in a different state? Different states have different tax laws. Investigate!

We are a country of impatient people. "Dear Lord, give me patience and do it right now." Slow down. Smell the money saved. We really don't need E-mail. Stamps are much cheaper. (How much did your computer cost?) It is fun to have the mailman bring you a letter. Eliminate all unnecessary expenses. Even eliminate some of what you have previously considered necessary.

Grocery shop on discount days. It's painless and who cares what day you buy your weekly food supply?

Wait until the end of the season to have your winter clothes cleaned to put away. There is generally a special at your cleaners. Utilize any specials they have during the year.

Buy clothes in the off-season on sale. The stores still make a profit and you save a bundle. Surely you always buy classic styles that look good year in and year out. Do you really care whether trousers have pleats or not this season? No one is likely to mistake you for the Duke of Windsor.

Plant a vegetable and herb garden. (Use that compost.) You not only get exercise, you get very inexpensive food.

HINT: The more you can do for yourself, the more you save.

Pay to *exercise?* I think not. If you must have the companionship of sweaty people working a machine, that is your choice and expense. Yard care will give you a good cardiovascular workout and it's free. Think of pulling weeds as helping to develop your abs. If you don't have a yard, help an elderly neighbor or friend with theirs. Then, besides the health benefits and savings, you are adding stars to your crown in heaven. Do take care of your body and appearance. You don't want to look like ten miles of bad road.

Wash and clean your cars. Whether you pay two or twenty dollars to have it done, your own driveway and hose is cheaper. Wax them yourself and you will really save money.

Keep a record of the money you save by doing these chores. They will cease to be chores and you will be amazed at the money you are saving. It will help to reinforce these frugal pursuits.

CHAPTER 10

NITTY PICKY
WAYS TO SAVE

"If it's yellow, let it mellow. If it's brown, flush it down." This slogan was popular in California years ago during a drought. It is a water and money saver, but the aesthetics leave something to be desired.

Drive around in the fall and find pine needles that people have raked to the street or bagged. Or, help friends rake and bag theirs if they don't use it. It is great mulch for azaleas or any acid loving shrub. No need to buy what nature gives you.

After Halloween, there are often bales of straw put curbside. These bales were used in Halloween displays along with pumpkins and cornstalks. Take a bale or two home to use in the spring if you plan to reseed a part of your lawn.

Recycle. Recycle.

Be really, really cheap. Use paper napkins more than once. A lady who did so died a millionaire. No guarantee you will, but this type of thinking helps to get you there.

Zip lock bags, plastic coated paper plates, plastic utensils can all be washed and reused. Some items are even labeled "disposable/reusable." That's a no-brainer. Reuse and reuse.

Save paper clips that come in the mail and use them when needed. I have never had to buy any.

Don't rush to the cleaners. Wash your wool sweaters after you learn the proper techniques. In the summer, brush and air your winter coats and scarves in the sun. Let the warmth and elbow grease save cleaning costs.

Discontinue newspapers when you are out of town. They don't accumulate and let burglars know you aren't home. You don't need to bother a neighbor to take them in. Your subscription date moves forward and you save.

HINT: Yesterday's news is just that.

In our diminished income years, wedding invitations can prove to be an expense that eats into our food budget. My mother used to say that she spent the first half of her life collecting things and the second half wondering what to do with them. Herein lies a solution to the RSVP (Remember to Send the Wedding Present). Find a "lovely something" of yours, clean it up and send it on its way.

HINT: To cull your
possessions is always a plus.

When leaving the house for a vacation or even for a few hours, if a storm is predicted, make sure you unplug your TV, CD player and anything that might be damaged.

HINT: An ounce of prevention
can save big bucks and trouble.

Some Obvious No No's

Don't use a check cashing service.

Don't use ATM cards that charge a fee.

Don't bank at a place that charges you to talk with a teller. (Are these banks crazy?!)

Don't trade at a gas station that charges you for the air you put in your tires.

HINT: Just because certain
strange procedures exist doesn't
mean we have to use them.

Iron tissue paper that comes to you in boxes or gift bags. Don't buy it. Of course, reuse the colorful gift bags friends give you with presents and wine. They cost two to five dollars and can be used over and over again. (Your friends will think you are a big spender.)

Don't waste money buying plastic liners for your wastebaskets. Use the plastic or paper bags provided for carrying your groceries. Your liners are then free. Paper bags hold more trash.

Some advice when eating out. As we reach our platinum years (white hair time), we can't or don't need to eat as much as we did. Take what is left over for the next day. You don't have to make up a dog's name. "Old Spot will love this steak." The restaurants just throw out left over food. Whether you also pocket an occasional pack of sugar or crackers is up to you.

One elderly couple, in our town, could be seen at public events, receptions, art exhibits, anywhere food was served. They rarely missed one. The lady always had her oversized lined purse into which a sampling of the food was placed as they worked their way from table to table. They ate their evening meal at the function and their "purse meal" was utilized later. I sincerely hope your circumstances or penurious nature don't require such a measure, but it is "food for thought."

When the bar of soap is really too small to use, press it on top of a new bar and you will use it all.

When you pour what you think is the last of the liquor from the bottle, cap it and store it upside down for twenty-four hours. Lo and behold, you have almost another drink.

HINT: A jigger saved
is a jigger earned.

If there is a store in your town that sells ham and slices of ham, ask for a ham bone to use for making soup. There may be a minimal charge or it may be free. There is often enough ham left on the bone for a meal and some sandwiches. You can still make delicious soup or red beans and rice with what's left.

Take food in the car on road trips. I get hungry about the time I leave the city limits. This way, you can eat and drive. You don't waste time stopping and looking for a place to eat. Guess what? You have saved two things...time and money.

On a long road trip, pack a cooler of food. You can eat more economically in your room. Potato chips, cokes, cookies, candy and nuts taken with you are much cheaper than from vending machines or in the courtesy (make that expensive) bar.

After getting a number from information (which is expensive enough) the phone service wants to dial the number for you for an additional fee. Have your fingers suddenly fallen off? I don't think so. Spend money because you are too lazy to dial a number? Get real!

When you leave a room, do the Lyndon Johnson thing. (When he was in the White House ... Yes, that one.) Turn off the lights. Your furniture isn't afraid of the dark and you save money.

When you rent a video, the rental time is usually three to five days. Normally, you will view it only once. Get on a program with friends and pass it along and share the cost. You will be getting great movies at a very reduced rate.

The experts tell you the temperatures to keep your heating and cooling systems. Their suggestions are usually too high and too low. In the winter, wear sweaters instead of supporting your local utility system. In the warmer months, open doors and windows. God will send you cross ventilation and you will save, save, save.

I bet you have a few Christmas cards left over each year. It's hard to guess the number you need and they are sold in lots of a certain size anyway. One year, just collect the old cards and use them. You probably have enough for that year. Trust me. Your friends won't remember they have received a similar one before.

If you feel compelled to buy birthday, get-well, whatever kind of cards; instead of writing on them, write on a plain piece of paper and enclose it in the card. Your friends not only get your good wishes, they have a clean card they can send someone. They will love your thoughtfulness. Better yet, forget the card and write a note. It is more personal and will be greatly appreciated because so few people do it.

Telephone calls are expensive and getting more so despite what the companies' T.V. ads say. There are more add-on charges each month than calls I make. (Only a slight exaggeration.) Remember stamps?

If you are calling long distance and no one answers, hang up before the answering machine clicks on. If you must leave a message, don't have verbal diarrhea. Learn to be succinct. The military says to give only name, rank and serial number. Follow this good advice when leaving a message. Give name, time, date and your number. Talk is not cheap.

When talking with folks long distance, have a clock or watch in view. Maybe what you say is worth lots of bucks, but my thoughts aren't that important. I don't know any calling plan that beats a 39¢ stamp.

Paperback books cost what hardback books used to cost. Swap paperbacks at second-hand stores. It helps to clean your shelves and to get new reading material.

Use tea bags more than once. It works and why not?

Don't drink a lot of sodas (belly wash) or fruit flavored drinks. Substitute water. It is much cheaper and better for you. It will also help with the weight reduction plan you should be considering. For heaven's sake, don't buy bottled water. If your water tastes so bad that even with a slice of lemon, you don't want to drink it, you should move. Bottled water doesn't even give you fluoride protection.

A word of caution. Generic drugs taken by mouth are cheaper than brand name ones. The media and your pharmacist will tell you so. However, they do not always contain the total amount of the drug that a non-generic contains. Therefore, you might not be getting the proper dose of the medicine you need. Check with your trusted pharmacist on this one.

Don't buy flowers to decorate your home. Grow them. Use leaves and parts of bushes in arrangements. Be imaginative. Be cheap.

Add milk to the "empty" chocolate syrup container. Shake and you have another drink or two.

You are at home. Brush your teeth more often. Dental work is expensive.

CHAPTER 11

DO UNTO OTHERS

Help your fellow man and woman. The more you give, the more you get.

Your time is free. No demands. No *must-do* things. No schedule. No deadlines, as you had at work. But beware. The "time users" are all around you. Just waiting to pounce. Set your own pace.

A truly wonderful way to use some of your time is to help others.

Visit a sick friend. Take food, or books, or items that might be of interest. For example, when a philatelist friend was recovering from surgery, I took him some old stamp albums we had around the house. I was hoping he might find a treasure. Perhaps a double reverse, upside down, Morivan silver print...yeah, right! He didn't find anything of value, but it gave him something to do that he enjoyed.

Take magazines or candy. Just visit. Reestablish old friendships. During our working and child rearing years, we often lose contact with friends while we car pool and climb the corporate ladder. Get back in touch. Few of us have more friends than we need or want.

How green are her eyes? It's fine to help your fellow man, but your wife may not like for you to help your fellow woman too often. At our age, there are more widows than married folk. What you fix for a neighbor lady is fine; if you don't make a career of it. Wives are protective. Sometimes they need to be. You've made it together this long. You really have no need to add stress to the next number of years. Be helpful, not tempted. Enough said.

Drive friends to and from the hospital if they are having treatments or tests. It is a lonely and scary time. Stay with them during those long hours of chemotherapy. Their alternative to your company is daytime T.V. No one, friend or foe, should be subjected to that mess.

When your friend closes his eyes, it's time for you to stop talking and to read that book you brought along. Just by being there, you help. Make follow-up visits when your friend is at home. Friends who have had cancer operations or other major surgery are evaluating their mortality. (One friend says there is no minor surgery, only minor surgeons!) They often have trouble getting their lives back to normal.

Hospital stays tend to make one withdrawn and create a feeling of depression and dependence. When they are able, take them out for a drive or to lunch. Early public appearances and outings after operations and treatments are the hardest. Help to break the cycle of their illness. Both parties profit. Our turn may come.

HINT: Always have younger friends, so that someone is able to tote and fetch for you.

Take people to and from the airport. Or leave their car there for them on the day of their return. It is easier than meeting them since flights are often delayed. It will save your friends (and you, when they reciprocate) a passel of money in parking fees.

Help around your church or synagogue. Invariably, something needs to be fixed, painted or trimmed. The same is true for any number of community organizations in which you may have an interest.

If you tend to be insular and self-centered, now is the time to look around. There are always people better off and worse off. You have an opportunity to broaden your vision and your life.

Helping others doesn't have to require money. Just being an interested friend is a gift. Get out of yourself. Smile more often. (People will wonder what you are up to!) The world awaits your help and thoughtfulness. Get happy.

CHAPTER 12

SUMMARY

Retirement is all about money and time. The key to a good retirement is to be frugal and to zealously guard your time. It's yours to use or lose. "How do you stay busy?" you will be asked. "What do you do with your time?" You have no more control over time now than when you were working. It moves along quite nicely without any help from you. Don't pack your bags for a guilt trip. Just smile and say, "Life is good." It has been said that "in retirement the thing I miss the most is my weekend." Not so. Everyday is a weekend. It's just hard sometimes to know *what* day it is.

HINT: Smile and enjoy.

People continue to worry about my wife. They fear the worse and are dreading the day when their spouse retires. My wife, bless her, just says retirement is good. But, then we both try hard to make it work.

Your retirement should be a treat for your spouse. Don't make life harder for her or you. Don't act out in such a way that your wife needs to quote H. L. Mencken, "A man may be a fool and not know it, but not if he is married."

HINT: In real estate, it's location, location, location. In retirement, it's accommodation, accommodation, accommodation.

You will be able to add many ideas to this guide. That is the point of it; to get you thinking and planning. Your options are unlimited. Do nothing or much. Your personality and desires will dictate your activities. Your time is precious. No one can tell you how much you have left. Use each day as if it were your last. Take nothing for granted. Seize all of life. You're free!

William J. Cone

Lightning Source UK Ltd.
Milton Keynes UK
05 December 2009

147130UK00001B/100/A